Jack
Love
Nannie
xx oo

happiness is ...

HAVING THE
BEST MOM!

happiness is ...

200 things i love about m♥m

Lisa Swerling & Ralph Lazar

CHRONICLE BOOKS

SAN FRANCISCO

*how you make special
occasions even more special*

a care package
from home

being a genius in your eyes

seeing you look
beautiful

when you slip
me money when
Dad's not looking

a comfortable
silence

✓doing a project
together

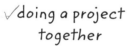

a mom wake-up call

reading together

constant
encouragement

how you "inspire"
me to clean my room

asking for a snack and
you treating me to a
five-course meal

the smell of your
perfume

when you sneak a
treat into my bag

acting like crazy people

giving you something
really special

seeing the world with you

being your tech
support

how you're a better
cook than you take
credit for

feeling inspired
by you

mom therapy

seeing how much
you worry about me

the smells of home

a long beach walk
together

our inside jokes

*having you there for
the big stuff and the
small stuff*

your positivity

being spoiled

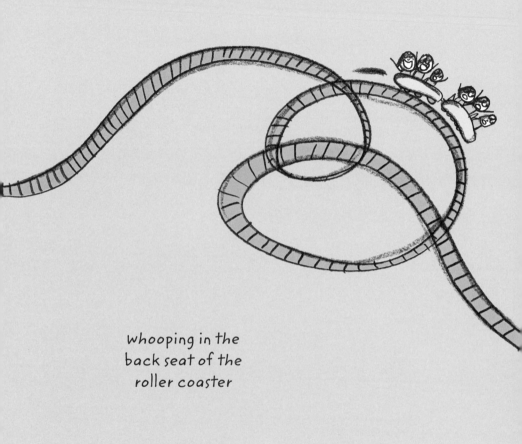

whooping in the
back seat of the
roller coaster

you putting an extra
blanket on me

a quick call about
nothing in particular

when you let me win

coffee and
a catch up

seeing myself in you

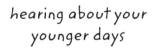

hearing about your
younger days

bedtime stories

finding a box of my toys in your attic

getting help with my homework

realizing you kept all the cards I've made you

how you push me to work harder

falling asleep on
your lap

hot soup and warm
conversation

*reminiscing over
my baby photos*

the perfect way you make the bed

learning your secret recipes

hanging out
in our pj's

building sand castles

making you a present

a shopping spree with you

being the best
of friends

learning from your
example

when you spoil me
on sick days

when you display my
art as if it's a Picasso

appreciating all you
do for our family

having time, just the
two of us

sharing a sense
of humor

hearing stories
about my childhood

a piggyback ride

making you coffee, just the way you like it

beating the master

making dreams a reality

when people say we look alike

bringing you breakfast in bed

*hearing about
the day I was
born*

taking you out to dinner

discovering a whole
new side of you

rocking out together

a huge "HELLO!"
when you get home
from work

having you as my go-to guru

watching you make
a house a home

planning an
adventure

recreating your signature dishes

vacationing
together

snuggly sleepovers

having you there in
an emergency

being amazed
by your talent

looking at photos of
you as a kid

hugs that make
everything ok

building something
together

finding magic in
the everyday

feeling safe by
your side

hearing you sing at
the top of your voice

always
making up

our movie marathons

having the best time
doing absolutely nothing

when you let me
show off

telling you every
little detail

feeling you can protect
me from anything

sharing your
tears of joy

a sing-along for two

finding your
gray hairs

trying new foods
together

knowing we have
a unique bond

enjoying the same hobby

mixing your
favorite drink

seeing you arrive at just
the right moment

having a whole
conversation with
just one look

cracking up when
I remember
something you said

sharing our favorite
takeout

when you sing songs from
my childhood

how you manage to fit it all in

watching you cook

when you encourage
me to achieve my
dreams

holidays together

a special night out

when you help me pack
even though you don't
want me to go

being far away but feeling
close at the same time

having someone
I can rant to
without restraint

when your mom's
the boss

bringing out your
silly side

when you answer my calls in
the middle of the night

smoothies à la mom

your driving lessons

when you teach me
cool things

solving problems
over dinner

your can-do attitude

facing the world
together

when you impress
my friends

when people tell me I take after you

when you make wishes come true

planning trips to
see you

when you push me to
try something new

listening to your
favorite music from
back in the day

knowing not to bug you
when you're concentrating

making things
with you

when you pick up all the
essentials

wearing an outfit that
you bought for me

how you sacrifice your
own comfort for mine

having the same
taste in movies

your silly
nicknames

my shnooky
shnooky
wookums

sharing problems
that only a mom
would understand

sharing giggly gossip

introducing you to
the person I love

when you read to me

loving the same band

being old enough to keep up with you

how you always
know just what to do

having you around
when I'm not
feeling well

gifts from you in my grown-up
Christmas stocking

feeling your
constant love

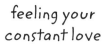

go get
'em, tiger

hearing words of
encouragement on my
way out the door

watching you
triumph

imitating your catchphrases

when you remind me to
dress warmly

having a patient
teacher

picking you up at
the airport

when you call me
by my childhood
nickname

watching you do
your makeup

saying "good-bye"
and then chatting for
another half hour

your healing powers

laughing around the
dinner table

friending you on
social media

being treated like
a grown-up

knowing how much
my friends like you

sharing indulgences

never-ending
online chats

reading articles you
cut out for me

when you reveal
hidden talents

when you give me the heart
of your artichoke

being goofballs

our little adventures

making memories

trusting your sage advice

trying out your awesome dance moves

family traditions through the years

your selflessness

chatting about anything and everything

lazy cozy afternoons

calling you first when
I have important news

when you tuck me in,
even as an adult

sitting down to your
delicious cooking

knowing you love me
no matter what

learning about
my heritage

finding my old school
photos tucked in
your drawer

surprising you with
a cup of tea

when you're my #1 fan

going out
to celebrate

showing you how to use
your phone correctly

how you always find
the perfect gift

how you think everything I do is fantastic

our little rituals

a family vacation

being creative together

being cared for

when you
recommend a book
and I love it too

mom hugs

still holding hands when
we cross the street

tickle sneak-attacks

getting real letters
from you

just us and
a pot of tea

a shoulder to cry on

becoming friends

finding the money you
snuck into my bag

running errands together

making you proud

"borrowing"
your shoes

hearing you tell that
same story over and
over again

unconditional love

ISBN 978-1-4521-4265-4
Manufactured in China.

Design by Lisa Swerling and Ralph Lazar

10 9 8 7 6 5 4 3 2

Chronicle Books LLC
680 Second Street
San Francisco, CA 94107
www.chroniclebooks.com